MW01130285

T 59355

08-01

The Girlhood Diary of

Louisa May Alcott,

1843-1846:

Writings of a Young Author

Edited by Kerry A. Graves

Content Consultant:
Jan Turnquist, Executive Director,
and the Orchard House Staff
Orchard House Museum, Concord, Massachusetts

Blue Earth Books

an imprint of Capstone Press
Mankato, Minnesota

Blue Earth Books are published by Capstone Press
151 Good Counsel Drive, P.O. Box 669, Mankato, Minnesota 56002
http://www.capstone-press.com

Library of Congress Cataloging-in-Publication Data
Alcott, Louisa May, 1832–1888.
  The girlhood diary of Louisa May Alcott, 1843–1846: writings of a young author/edited by
Kerry A. Graves.
    p. cm. – (Diaries, letters, and memoirs)
    Includes bibliographical references (p. 31) and index.
    Summary: Excerpts from the girlhood diary of Louisa May Alcott, describing her family life, lessons,
and experiences on a communal farm in the 1840s. Includes sidebars, activities, and a timeline related to
this era.
    ISBN 0-7368-0599-0
    1. Alcott, Louisa May, 1832–1888—Diaries—Juvenile literature. 2. Alcott, Louisa May,
1832–1888—Childhood and youth—Juvenile literature. 3. Authors, American—19th century—
Diaries—Juvenile literature. [1. Alcott, Louisa May, 1832–1888—Childhood and youth. 2. Authors,
American. 3. Women—Biography. 4. Diaries. 5. United States—Social life and customs—1783–1865.]
I. Graves, Kerry. II. Series.
PS1018.A427 2001
818'.403—dc21
[B]   00–036036

Editorial credits

Editor: Kay M. Olson
Designer: Heather Kindseth
Illustrator: Linda Clavel
Photo researchers: Heidi Schoof and
    Kimberly Danger
Artistic effects: Louise Sturm-McLaughlin

Photo credits

Orchard House Museum, cover, 6, 7 (all),
9, 12 (right), 16 (all), 27 (bottom), 28 (all),
29 (bottom); Fruitlands Museums,
Harvard, Massachusetts, cover background,
11, 12 (left), 18; Gregg Andersen, 14, 17;
Concord Free Public Library 27 (top),
Stock Montage, 29 (top).

1 2 3 4 5 6 06 05 04 03 02 01

CONTENTS

Editor's Note

The Diaries, Letters, and Memoirs series introduces real young people from different time periods in American history. Whenever possible, the diary entries in this book appear word for word as they were written in the young person's original diary. Because the diary appears in its original form, you will notice some misspellings and mistakes in grammar. To clarify the writer's meaning, corrections or explanations within a set of brackets sometimes follow the misspellings and mistakes.

This book contains only portions of Louisa May Alcott's girlhood diary. Text sometimes has been removed from the individual diary entries. In these cases, you will notice three dots in a row, which are called ellipses. Ellipses show that words or sentences are missing from a text.

The original pages of Louisa May Alcott's girlhood diary have been lost over the years. Passages of her diary presented here are from Ednah Cheney's 1889 book, *Louisa May Alcott: Her Life, Letters, and Journals,* as well as *Transcendental Wild Oats and Fragments from the Fruitlands Diaries,* currently held at the Fruitlands Museum in Harvard, Massachusetts. We extend special thanks to the Fruitlands Museum and to Dr. John Pratt on behalf of the literary heirs of Louisa May Alcott for permission to reprint portions of her diary.

" . . . *things have gone on so swimmingly of late I
don't know who I am. A year ago I had no publisher &
went begging with my wares, now three have asked me for
something, several papers are ready to print my contributions . . .
There is a sudden hoist for a meek & lowly scribbler who was
told to 'stick to her teaching,' & never had a literary friend to
lend a helping hand! Fifteen years of hard grubbing may be
coming to something after all, & I may yet 'pay all the debts, fix
the house, send May to Italy & keep the old folks cosy,' as I've
said I would so long yet so hopelessly.*"

—Louisa May Alcott

Louisa May Alcott
The Girlhood Diary of a Young Author

In 1843, Louisa May Alcott wrote in her journal, "I should like to be famous." Today, people know her best as the author of *Little Women*. Louisa based this well-known novel on her family.

On November 29, 1832, Louisa was born in Germantown, Pennsylvania. Her father, Bronson, was a teacher and a philosopher. Louisa's mother, Abigail, was the daughter of a respected Boston family. Bronson and Abigail were the models for Mr. March and Marmee, the parents in *Little Women*. Louisa's three sisters, Anna, Elizabeth, and May, were fictionalized as Meg, Beth, and Amy March in the novel. The book's main character, Jo, was based on Louisa herself. The Alcotts' friends and relatives were other characters in the novel.

Louisa's family and the imaginary Marches were similar in many ways. Both families believed society placed too much importance on money and possessions. Like the Alcotts, the Marches lived simply and helped less fortunate people. They wanted to end slavery in the Southern states, and they respected nature.

The Alcotts also were very different from the March family. The Alcotts often moved to find work and an affordable home. Louisa's father was an innovative teacher who did not earn very much money. The Alcotts often were in debt and relied on others to help them. Louisa's mother worked hard to feed the family. Louisa worried about her family's well being. She wanted to become rich to help her mother.

Louisa's parents believed education was very important. They made sure their daughters studied wherever the family lived. But the Alcott girls rarely attended

Louisa May was the second of Bronson and Abigail's four daughters. She modeled the character Jo in Little Women *on herself.*

Louisa's sisters, Elizabeth, Anna, and May, were represented by the characters Beth, Meg, and Amy in Little Women.

a school. Their father and his philosopher friends tutored the girls at home. Louisa and her sisters studied nature, religion, good behavior, music, and academics such as history and math.

Louisa learned about responsibility through hard work. In 1843, the Alcotts lived on a communal farm called Fruitlands near Harvard, Massachusetts. As many as ten other people lived and worked with them. The farm was designed to provide food for all its members. Everyone did daily household or farm chores, including the Alcott children. Even so, Fruitlands failed that winter. The Alcotts lived with friends and rented rooms until they moved to Hillside in Concord, Massachusetts, in April 1845.

Louisa's parents kept journals and encouraged their children to do so as well. The Alcotts did not keep their journals private from one another. Instead, family members read each other's journals and wrote notes in them. In 1868, Louisa used these journal entries and her memories to write *Little Women*.

Louisa believed her family life should be private. She did not enjoy fame and did not like to sign autographs. As an adult, Louisa read her journals and destroyed many pages from them. The entries included here are taken from those she kept. From these surviving entries, we can learn about Louisa's family and childhood. We might also recognize some events from the pages of *Little Women*.

The Diary of Louisa May Alcott

Friday 4 [August 1843]—

After breakfast I washed the dishes and then had my lessons. Father and
Mr Kay and Mr Lane went to the Shakers and did not return till evening.
After my lessons I sewed till dinner. When dinner was over I had a bath, and
then went to Mrs Williards. When I came home I played till supper time, after
which I read a little in Oliver Twist [by Charles Dickens], and when I had
thought a little I went to bed. I have spent quite a pleasant day.

*The Alcotts moved frequently during Louisa's childhood, but they usually lived in or
near the town of Concord, Massachusetts.*

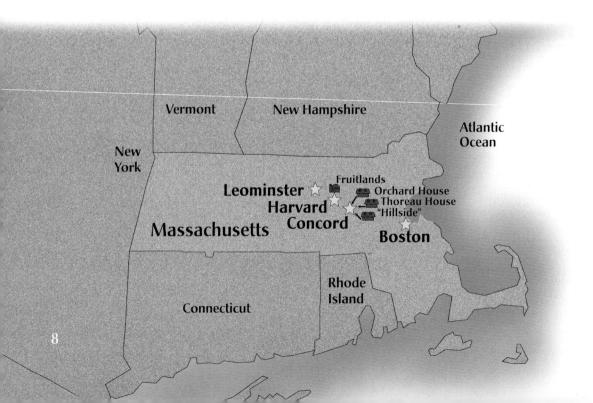

Little Women

Little Women is a lively story of family life. The novel portrays the Marches, a New England family in the 1860s. Mr. March, the father of four daughters, is a chaplain serving in the Union army during the Civil War (1861–1865). Mrs. March, called Marmee by her daughters, is calm and capable during her husband's absence. Meg, the oldest daughter, is well-behaved and pretty. Jo, the next oldest sister, is high-spirited and temperamental. Beth is the frail, quiet sister. Amy, the youngest of the girls, is rambunctious and a little spoiled.

The family is poor, but the four March sisters manage to have fun despite their hardships. The girls play pranks, act out plays, and share dreams with each other. As they grow from girls into women, the March sisters struggle through hardships and celebrate their achievements. Meg marries and becomes the mother of twins. Jo, the March sister Louisa based on herself, becomes a writer. Sadly, Beth dies before she grows to adulthood. Young Amy becomes an artist and finds romance with an old friend from the girls' childhood.

G. E. Morris

LITTLE WOMEN

OR,

MEG, JO, BETH AND AMY

BY LOUISA M. ALCOTT

ILLUSTRATED BY MAY ALCOTT

BOSTON
ROBERTS BROTHERS
1869

They all drew to the fire, mother in the big chair, with Beth at her feet; Meg and Amy perched on either arm of the chair, and Jo leaning on the back. — Page 12.

The Shakers

In the mid-1700s, a small group of Quakers in Manchester, England, would shake, dance, and shout during religious services. Most Quakers thought this groups' actions were radical and called them Shaking Quakers, or Shakers. The Shakers broke away from the Quaker religion.

A woman named Ann Lee was one of these Shakers. Ann Lee told other Shakers that Jesus had anointed her with the spirit of Christ. She said God was both Father and Mother, not three male persons in one God. She believed that men and women were equal.

She told other Shakers that men and women should live together as brothers and sisters and not as husbands and wives. English townsfolk did not like someone preaching against the Bible's command to "multiply and replenish the earth." They had Ann Lee put in jail to punish her for preaching her beliefs.

When she was released from prison in 1774, Ann Lee and some of her followers moved to New York. They wanted to be free of religious persecution in England. The first Shaker community in the United States was a communal farm in Watervliet, New York. Community members produced their own food and lived without luxuries. They shared all their belongings. Men and women lived in separate buildings or in separate rooms of large dwelling houses.

By the 1830s, more than 5,000 Shakers lived in the United States. After 1860, interest in the religion declined, largely because Shakers did not believe in marriage or in traditional family life. Today only one active Shaker community exists in the world. Located in Maine, the Sabbathday Lake Shaker Village contains 18 buildings on 1,800 acres (7.2 hectares) of land. Members maintain a tree farm, apple orchard, gardens, hay fields, pastures, and a variety of livestock. They also make baskets, weave, and make some small wooden items. The community supports itself in part by selling these items.

People in the Harvard Shaker Village in the 1900s followed the same traditions and way of life as the Shakers that Bronson Alcott visited. This religious group lived simply and believed in hard work. Shakers were known for their farming skills.

Tuesday 8—

After I had bathed and dressed, I came to breakfast. After breakfasting I washed the dishes and then went berrying with Anna and William [Lane] we did not return untill dinner time. After dinner, I read and made clothes for my doll and had a bath. I sewed till 5 oclock, and went to walk. Lizzy and [I] played out till supper was ready. After supper I washed the dishes, and went to bed.

Sunday 28—

   After breakfast I read till 9 oclock and Father read a Parable called Nathan. and I liked it very well he then asked us all what faults we watted [wanted] to get rid of I said Impatience, and Mr Lane selfwill. We had a dinner of bread and water after which I read thought and walked till supper.

Wednesday 30—

   After breakfast I washed the dishes and then Mother Anna Miss Robie and Harriet and myself went to Leominster to see a house which Father thinks of buying I liked it pretty well and I enjoyed my ride very much. we did not return till evening.

   The people at Fruitlands lived according to a schedule. Each person had certain chores and everyone was expected to do their work at regular times each day. Louisa and her sisters were expected to follow this schedule of work, lessons, meals, and recreation time.

Life at Fruitlands

In 1842, Bronson Alcott met Charles Lane and Henry Wright during a trip to England. Like Mr. Alcott, the men were teachers and philosophers who admired the Shakers' organized lifestyle and farming methods. The men began to plan Fruitlands. Mr. Alcott returned from England to his family that October and brought Mr. Lane, his son William, and Mr. Wright. In May of 1843, Mr. Lane bought land for the Fruitlands community. A month later, the Alcotts, the Lanes, and Mr. Wright moved and began fixing buildings and planting gardens.

Fruitlands did not have running water or electricity. People carried water to the house for bathing, cleaning, and cooking. During winter, community members chopped wood to fuel the stove and heat the house. The Alcott girls cleaned and filled oil lamps each day.

At Fruitlands, Louisa and her sisters spent their days with lessons, chores, and recreation. The Alcotts used a chart to organize all daily activities. At five o'clock in the morning they woke up, bathed, and then spent two hours doing household chores. They dusted, swept, cooked, and washed dishes. The girls studied until noon and took a rest after dinner. In the afternoon, the girls did errands and chores. They sometimes read or sewed. Their favorite activities were performing plays and hiking in the woods.

Fruitlands members had many beliefs that affected their everyday lives. They did not wear wool clothing because wool is made from the fleece of animals. They did not wear cotton clothes because cotton was picked by slaves, and Fruitlands members opposed slavery. Instead, they made their clothes from linen, a cloth made from the flax plant. Fruitlands members did not eat meat or other animal products such as eggs or milk. They only allowed grains, fruits, and vegetables in their strict vegetarian diet. Water was the only beverage they drank.

September 1st.—

I rose at five and had my bath. I love cold water! Then we had our singing-lesson with Mr. Lane. After breakfast I washed dishes, and ran on the hill till nine, and had some thoughts, — it was so beautiful up there. Did my lessons, — wrote and spelt and did sums; and Mr. Lane read a story, "The Judicious Father": How a rich girl told a poor girl not to look over the fence at the flowers, and was cross to her because she was unhappy. The father heard her do it, and made the girls change clothes. The poor one was glad to do it, and he told her to keep them. But the rich one was very sad; for she had to wear the old ones a week, and after that she was good to shabby girls. I liked it very much, and I shall be kind to poor people.

Father asked us what was God's noblest work. Anna said *men*, but I said *babies*. Men are often bad; babies never are. We had a long talk, and I felt better after it, and *cleared up*.

We had bread and fruit for dinner. I read and walked and played till supper-time. We sung in the evening. As I went to bed the moon came up very brightly and looked at me. I felt sad because I have been cross today, and did not mind Mother. I cried, and then I felt better, and said that piece from Mrs. Sigourney, "I must not tease my mother." I get to sleep saying poetry, —I know a great deal.

Thursday, 14th.—

Mr. Parker Pillsbury came, and we talked about the poor slaves. I had a music lesson with Miss P. I hate her, she is so fussy. I ran in the wind and played be a horse, and had a lovely time in the woods with Anna and Lizzie. We were fairies, and made gowns and paper wings. I "flied" the highest of all . . . It rained when I went to bed, and made a pretty noise on the roof.

14

Slavery and the Abolition Movement

Before the Civil War, many Southerners in the United States made their living by growing cotton and tobacco on large farms called plantations. Slaves picked these crops by hand.

Southerners believed slavery was necessary for their farms and plantations to survive. The Alcotts and other abolitionists wanted to end slavery in the United States. Religious groups such as the Quakers believed slavery was wrong. Some New England states abolished slavery before 1804. In 1821, William Lloyd Garrison started an anti-slavery newspaper called the *Liberator*. This publication urged people to take a stand against slavery.

Abolitionists did more than speak out and write against slavery. They worked to elect other abolitionists to state and national offices. They encouraged the government to change laws. Abolitionists helped slaves escape to free states or to Canada. Slavery officially ended in 1865, when the Thirteenth Amendment to the U.S. Constitution was adopted.

Sunday, 24th.—

Father and Mr. Lane have gone to N[ew]. H[ampshire]. to preach. It was very lovely . . . Anna and I got supper. In the eve I read "Vicar of Wakefield" [by Oliver Goldsmith]. I was cross to-day, and I cried when I went to bed. I made good resolutions, and felt better in my heart. If I only *kept* all I make, I should be the best girl in the world. But I don't, and so am very bad.

The Little Women *character Marmee was based on Louisa's mother, Abigail. The father in the novel, a Civil War Union chaplain, represented Bronson Alcott.*

October 8th.—

When I woke up, the first thought I got was, "It's Mother's birthday: I must be very good." I ran and wished her a happy birthday, and gave her my kiss. After breakfast we gave her our presents. I had a moss cross and a piece of poetry for her.

We did not have any school, and played in the woods and got red leaves. In the evening we danced and sung, and I read a story about "Contentment." I wish I was rich, I was good, and we were all a happy family this day . . .

Thursday, 12th.—

After lessons I ironed. We all went to the barn and husked corn. It was good fun. We worked till eight o'clock and had lamps. Mr. Russell came . . . I made a verse about sunset:—

Softly doth the sun descend
To his couch behind the hill,
Then, oh, then, I love to sit
On mossy banks beside the rill.

Anna thought it was very fine; but I did n't like it very well.

Make a Pressed Flower Card

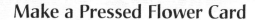

The Alcotts had a special mailbox for family members to send and receive messages. They made their own greeting cards and sometimes included poems in them.

What You Need:

newspaper

fresh flower blossoms

heavy books

white or colored unlined index
  card or construction paper

scissors (optional)

a small art paintbrush

craft glue that dries clear

tissues

paper cup

colored markers

What You Do:

1. Spread out newspapers on a flat surface.
2. Place flowers face down on the newspaper.
3. Cover the blossoms with several layers of newspaper. Do not bend the flowers.
4. Place heavy books over the newspapers.
5. After a week, remove the books and top layers of newspaper. Flowers that slide off the newspaper are ready to use. If flowers stick, repeat steps 3 to 5.
6. Fold the index card or paper in half to make a greeting card.
7. Choose pressed flowers for your card design. You may need scissors to trim the flower stems to make sure the flowers fit on the card.
8. Put some glue into the paper cup. Dip the paintbrush into the glue and brush a thin layer of glue on the back of a pressed flower. Be sure to coat the edges. Gently press the glued flower onto your card.
9. Add pressed flowers to finish your design. Blot any extra glue with a tissue.
10. Rinse the paintbrush in water to remove the glue while the card dries.
11. Write a message on the inside of your card with colored markers.

Friday, Nov. 2nd.—

Anna and I did the work. In the evening Mr. Lane asked us, "What is man?" These were our answers: A human being; an animal with a mind; a creature; a body; a soul and a mind. After a long talk we went to bed very tired . . .

Fruitlands members had not produced enough food to last through the coming winter. They had to find other homes. Mr. Lane believed Mrs. Alcott cared more about her family than the success of the group. He thought Mr. Alcott's wife and daughters were distracting him from his work. Mr. Alcott began to agree with Mr. Lane's opinions. The two men thought about leaving Fruitlands to start a new farm. The Alcotts discussed whether they should stay together or separate from Fruitlands. Mr. Alcott finally decided all the Alcotts would move together to a new home.

A Shaker sawmill stands next to the pond near Harvard, Massachusetts, where members of Fruitlands once lived. This photo was taken around 1900, about sixty years after the Alcott family and the others left Fruitlands.

Tuesday, 20th.—

I rose at five, and after breakfast washed the dishes, and then helped mother work. Miss P[age]. is gone, and Anna in Boston with Cousin Louisa. I took care of Abby (May) in the afternoon. In the evening I made some pretty things for my dolly. Father and Mr. L. had a talk, and father asked us if *we* saw any reason for us to separate. Mother wanted to, she is so tired. I like it, but not the school part or Mr. L.

Eleven years old. Thursday, 29th.—

It was Father's and my birthday. We had some nice presents. We played in the snow before school. Mother read "Rosamond" [by Maria Edgeworth] when we sewed. Father asked us in the eve what fault troubled us most. I said my bad temper.

I told mother I liked to have her write in my book. She said she would put in more, and she wrote this to help me: —

DEAR LOUY,—Your handwriting improves very fast. Take pains and do not be in a hurry. I like to have you make observations about our conversations and your own thoughts. It helps you to express them and to understand your little self. Remember, dear girl, that a diary should be an epitome of your life. May it be a record of pure thought and good actions, then you will indeed be the precious child of your loving mother.

December 10th.—

I did my lessons, and walked in the afternoon. Father read to us in dear Pilgrim's Progress. Mr. L. was in Boston, and we were glad. In the eve father and mother and Anna and I had a long talk. I was very unhappy, and we all cried. Anna and I cried in bed, and I prayed God to keep us all together.

Saturday 23 [December]—

. . . I often wish I had a little brother but as I have not I shall try to be contented with what I have got, (for Mother often says if we are not contented with what we have got it will be taken away from us) and I think it is very true . . . in the evening we played cards and when I went to bed I felt happy for I had been obedient and kind to Father and Mother and gentle to my sisters, I wish I could be gentle always.

Sunday 24th—

After breakfast Father started for Boston, When he was gome [gone] I read and wrote till dinner after which I washed the dishes and then I made some presents for Christmass . . .

Christmass Day 1843, Monday 25—

I rose early and sat some looking at the Bon-bons in my stocking this is the piece of poetry which mother wrote for me

Christmass Rimes

Christmass is here
Louisa my dear
Then happy we'll be
Gladsome and free
God with you abide
With love for your guide
In time you'l go right
With heart and with might, . . .

CONCORD, Sunday.—

We all went into the woods to get moss for the *arbor* Father is making for *Mr. Emerson*. I miss Anna so much. I made two verses for her: —

TO ANNA.

Sister, dear, when you are lonely,
Longing for your distant home,
And the images of loved ones
Warmly to your heart shall come,
Then, mid tender thoughts and fancies
Let one fond voice say to thee,
"Ever when your heart is heavy,
Anna, dear, then think of me."
Think how we two have together
Journeyed onward day by day,
Joys and sorrows ever sharing,
While the swift years roll away.
Then may all the sunny hours
Of our youth rise up to thee,
And when your heart is light and happy,
Anna, dear, then think of me.

Wednesday.—

Read Martin Luther. A long letter from Anna. She sends me a picture of Jenny Lind, the great singer. She must be a happy girl. I should like to be famous as she is. Anna is very happy; and I don't miss her as much as I shall by and by in the winter.

. . . Had a splendid run, and got a box of cones to burn. Sat and heard the pines sing a long time. Read Miss Bremer's "Home" in the eve. Had good dreams, and woke now and then to think, and watch the moon. I had a pleasant time with my mind, for it was happy.

No diary entries exist for 1844.

John Bunyan's *Pilgrim's Progress*

Louisa's diary entries frequently mention *Pilgrim's Progress* by John Bunyan. In 1628, John Bunyan was born in Bedfordshire, England. In 1660, the English government forbade preaching in order to stop new churches from forming. Bunyan refused to obey the law and became a preacher. He was arrested for his beliefs and began writing *Pilgrim's Progress* while he was in prison.

Pilgrim's Progress is about a traveler named Christian. During Christian's journey, he meets characters with names such as Help, Mr. Worldly Wiseman, Goodwill, Simple, and Lord Hate-Good. Christian's experiences become religious lessons for the reader.

Pilgrim's Progress became one of the most popular books in England and the United States. It was one of Mr. Alcott's favorite childhood books. He often read *Pilgrim's Progress* to his girls as part of their lessons. Louisa copied favorite passages from the book into her journal. She also made *Pilgrim's Progress* an important part of the March girls' lessons in *Little Women*.

January, 1845, Friday.—

Did my lessons, and in the P. M. mother read "Kenilworth" [by Sir Walter Scott] to us while we sewed. It is splendid! I got angry and called Anna mean. Father told me to look out the word in the Dic[tionary]., and it meant "base," "contemptible." I was so ashamed to have called my dear sister that, and I cried over my bad tongue and temper.

We have had a lovely day. All the trees were covered with ice, and it shone like diamonds on fairy palaces. I made a piece of poetry about winter . . .

Wednesday.—

I am so cross I wish I had never been born.

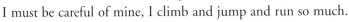

Thursday.—

Read the "Heart of Mid-Lothian," [by Sir Walter Scott] and had a very happy day. Miss Ford gave us a botany lesson in the woods. I am always good there. In the evening Miss Ford told us about the bones in our bodies, and how they get out of order. I must be careful of mine, I climb and jump and run so much.

I found this note from dear mother in my journal:—

MY DEAREST LOUY,—I often peep into your diary, hoping to see some record of more happy days. "Hope, and keep busy," dear daughter, and in all perplexity or trouble come freely to your

MOTHER

DEAR MOTHER,—You *shall* see more happy days, and I *will* come to you with my worries, for you are the best woman in the world.

L. M. A.

Louisa's Lessons

Mr. Alcott began teaching his daughters at home when they were very young. He had his own ideas about how to teach children. He thought memorizing information was not enough for a person to be educated. He wanted his children to be individuals and to study what was important to them. He wanted them to ask questions and to understand a subject. Mr. Alcott's lessons usually sounded more like conversations than lectures. Mr. Lane and the Alcott girls' other teachers used this same method.

Louisa and her sisters learned about reading, writing, grammar, mathematics, drawing, music, and geography. Their father also wanted them to learn about themselves and to be responsible. Louisa wrote in her journal about a conversational lesson with Mr. Lane:

"What virtues do you wish more of?" asks Mr. L.

I answer:—

Patience,	Love,	Silence,
Obedience,	Generosity,	Perseverance,
Industry,	Respect,	Self-denial.

"What vices less of?"

Idleness,	Willfulness,	Vanity,
Impatience,	Impudence,	Pride,
Selfishness,	Activity.	Love of cats.

How can you get what you need? By trying.
How do you try? By resolution and perseverance.
How gain love? By gentleness.
What is gentleness? Kindness, patience, and care for other people's feelings . . .

Tuesday.—

More people coming to live with us; I wish we could be together, and no one else. I don't see who is to clothe and feed us all, when we are so poor now. I was very dismal, and then went to walk and made a poem . . .

CONCORD, Thursday.—

I had an early run in the woods before the dew was off the grass. The moss was like velvet, and as I ran under the arches of yellow and red leaves I sang for joy, my heart was so bright and the world so beautiful. I stopped at the end of the walk and saw the sunshine out over the wide "Virginia meadows."

It seemed like going through a dark life or grave into heaven beyond. A very strange and solemn feeling came over me as I stood there, with no sound but the rustle of the pines, no one near me, and the sun so glorious, as for me alone. It seemed as if I *felt* God as I never did before, and I prayed in my heart that I might keep that happy sense of nearness in my life.

Thirteen Years Old.

Hillside. March, 1846,—

I have at last got the little room I have wanted so long, and am very happy about it. It does me good to be alone, and Mother has made it very pretty and neat for me. My work-basket and desk are by the window, and my closet is full of dried herbs that smell very nice. The door that opens into the garden will be very pretty in summer, and I can run off to the woods when I like.

I have made a plan for my life, as I am in my teens, and no more a child. I am old for my age, and don't care much for girl's things. People think I'm wild and queer; but Mother understands and helps me. I have not told any one about my plan; but I'm going to *be* good. I've made so many resolutions, and written sad notes, and cried over my sins, and it does n't seem to do any good! Now I'm going to *work really,* for I feel a true desire to improve, and be a help and comfort, not a care and sorrow, to my dear mother.

Starting Your Own Diary

Louisa's mother said a diary should be the epitome of one's life. Mrs. Alcott said Louisa would better understand herself by writing about her thoughts. Louisa used her diary to write about herself and record events in her life. She used her journal to compose poetry. All of these subjects are great topics for a journal. You can keep a journal to record your life and what happens in the world each day.

What You Need:

Paper: Use a blank book, a diary with a lock, or a notebook. Choose your favorite.

Pen: Choose a special pen or use different pens. You might want to use different colors to match your different moods.

Private time: Some people write before they fall asleep. Others write when they wake up. Be sure you have time to put down your thoughts without interruptions.

What You Do:

1. Begin each entry in your diary with the day and date. This step helps you remember when things happened. Later you can go back and read about what you did a week ago, a month ago, or a year ago.
2. Write about anything that interests you. Write about what you did today. Describe people you saw, what you studied, and songs you heard.
3. Write about your feelings. Describe what makes you happy or sad. Give your opinions about things you see, hear, or read.
4. Write in your diary regularly.

Afterword

Louisa carried out her resolution to "work really" and contribute to her family's income. As a teenager, Louisa worked as a teacher, governess, household servant, and seamstress. However, her favorite pastime was to write poems and stories. In 1850, Louisa's first poem was published.

Louisa was independent. From 1855 to 1856, she lived in Boston to try to earn more money. She lived in a boardinghouse, even though it was very unusual for an unmarried woman to live on her own. During the Civil War in 1862, Louisa moved to Washington, D.C., to work as an army nurse. She became seriously ill with typhoid pneumonia and returned home after only six weeks.

After recovering, Louisa wrote about her experiences as a nurse. A collection of stories called *Hospital Sketches* was her first big success. Her writing was in demand. In 1868, Louisa published *Little Women* and it became an instant favorite. The book was translated into many different languages and was published around the world.

Louisa supported her entire family with her earnings from writing. After *Little Women*, Louisa wrote *An Old Fashioned Girl*. In 1871, she wrote *Little Men*, followed by *Eight Cousins*, in 1874. Her novel *Rose in Bloom* was published in 1876, and in 1886 she wrote *Jo's Boys*.

Louisa supported many charitable causes, such as helping orphans and the poor. She worked with the temperance movement to try to stop the abuse of alcohol. Louisa also favored women's rights and was the first woman to register to vote in Concord.

Louisa's sister, May, had a baby daughter who she named Louisa May. The family called the baby Lulu. In 1879, May died and Louisa was named guardian of her sister's daughter, Lulu Nieriker. Louisa cared for her niece and continued publishing books. She never married. In 1888, at the age of 55, Louisa died in Roxbury, Massachusetts.

Louisa May Alcott had privacy in her bedroom (above) at Orchard House. Louisa lived in this house when she wrote Little Women. *Louisa was guardian of her niece, Louisa May Nieriker (right). The family gave the little girl the nickname Lulu.*

Timeline

Wagon trains begin to travel the Oregon Trail.

Ralph Waldo Emerson, a friend of the Alcott family, writes *Nature*.

James Marshall discovers gold in California's American River.

1831   1832   1835   1836   1840   1844

Louisa's sister Anna is born.

Louisa's sister Elizabeth is born.

Louisa's sister May is born.

Fruitlands fails and the Alcotts live with neighbors for the winter.

Louisa May Alcott is born in Germantown, Pennsylvania.

The U.S. Congress passes the Thirteenth Amendment to end slavery.

Alexander Graham Bell invents the telephone.

1858   **1865**   **1868**   **1876**   **1879**   **1888**

The Alcotts move to Orchard House in Concord, Massachusetts.

Louisa writes *Little Women*.

May dies and Louisa becomes the legal guardian of her niece Lulu.

March 4– Mr. Alcott dies. March 6– Louisa May Alcott dies at the age of 55 in Roxbury, Massachusetts.

LITTLE WOMEN

OR,

MEG, JO, BETH AND AMY

BY LOUISA M. ALCOTT

ILLUSTRATED BY MAY ALCOTT

BOSTON
ROBERTS BROTHERS
1869

29

Words to Know

anoint (uh-NOINT)—to honor someone during a religious ceremony by rubbing oil on his or her head

communal (kuh-MYOO-nuhl)—shared by several people

descend (di-SEND)—to climb down or go down to a lower level

doth (DOTH)—an old way of saying "do"

epitome (e-PIT-uh-mee)—a short description or statement of something

fault (FAWLT)—a weakness in a person's character

impudent (IM-pyuh-duhnt)—rude, bold, and outspoken

perplex (pur-PLEKS)—to make someone puzzled or unsure

perseverance (pur-suh-VEER-ance)—the act of trying over and over, even in the face of obstacles or difficulties

philosopher (fuh-LOSS-uh-fur)—a person who studies truth, wisdom, reality, and knowledge, and develops beliefs about how life should be lived

resolution (rez-uh-LOO-shuhn)—a promise to yourself that you will try hard to do something

rill (REHL)—a very small brook

self-denial (SELF-di-NYE-uhl)—limiting one's own needs and desires without help from others

typhoid pneumonia (TYE-foid noo-MOH-nyuh)—a serious disease with symptoms of high fever, diarrhea, and difficulty breathing

vegetarian (vej-uh-TER-ee-uhn)—someone who eats only plants and plant products and sometimes eggs or dairy products

Internet Sites

Concord Museum
http://www.concordmuseum.org

Orchard House (Alcott home)
http://www.louisamayalcott.org

Fruitlands Museums
http://www.fruitlands.org

The Wayside (Alcott's "Hillside")
http://www.nps.gov/mima/wayside

To Learn More

Altman, Linda Jacobs. *Slavery and Abolition: In American History.* Berkeley Heights, N.J.: Enslow Publishers, 1999.

Gormley, Beatrice. *Louisa May Alcott: Young Novelist.* Childhood of Famous Americans. New York: Aladdin Paperbacks, 1999.

McGill, Marci. *The Story of Louisa May Alcott, Determined Writer.* Famous Lives. Milwaukee: Gareth Stevens, 1996.

Ruth, Amy. *Louisa May Alcott.* Biography. Minneapolis: Lerner, 1999.

Wilber, Jessica. *Totally Private & Personal: Journaling Ideas for Girls and Young Women.* Minneapolis: Free Spirit Publishing, 1996.

Places to Write and Visit

Concord Museum
200 Lexington Road
Concord, MA 01742

Fruitlands Museums
102 Prospect Hill Road
Harvard, MA 01451

Orchard House (Alcott home)
399 Lexington Road
P.O. Box 343
Concord, MA 01742

The Wayside (Alcott's "Hillside")
455 Lexington Road
Concord, MA 01742

INDEX